Quickstart to Social Dancing

by Jeff Allen

Q Q S Publications
Cranston, RI

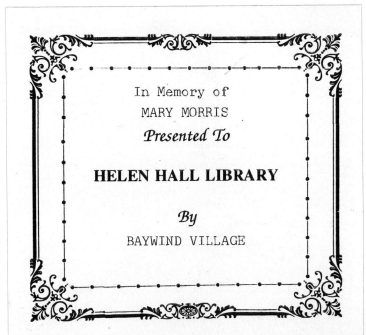

Allen, Jeffrey H.   a/k/a Allen, Jeff   1949 -
Quickstart to Social Dancing
Dancing   2. Ballroom Dancing   3. Social Activity   4. Wedding Advice & Information   I. Title

Published by:
Q Q S Publications
1315 New London Avenue
Cranston, RI 02920

Library of Congress Catalog Card Number: 96-093013

International Standard Book Number: 0-9654423-1-4

Second Edition, 1997
2-3-4-5-6-7-8-9-10-11-12
Printed in the United States of America

Quickstart to Social Dancing® and the Quickstart to Social Dancing Program® is a Registered Trade Mark

ABOUT THE AUTHOR

Jeff Allen is a graduate of the University of Rhode Island who has been self-employed since 1972. His interest in social and ballroom dancing began in 1960 with social dance classes in the Providence, Rhode Island area. By the late 70s Jeff's interest in competitive dancing began to consume all of his free time. At that time disco dancing and disco night club competition were the main thrusts of his dance activity. These dance competitions were held all over the New England and New York areas where Jeff won thousands of dollars competing. The disco craze soon subsided and Jeff's interest in competitive ballroom and Latin dancing was piqued. He began competing in national and international dance competitions. Jeff turned professional in July of 1984 after winning the gold closed level at the North American Championships. In that same year Jeff began traveling to Montreal, Quebec, a mecca of ballroom dancing, for teacher training and competitive dancing. This journey continued every four weeks for three and one-half years. During and following that time, Jeff finished in fourth place in the Canadian Provincial Basic and the Standard Professional Latin Championships. He also won the New England Professional American Smooth Championships, finished second in the Rising Star Closed Latin North American Championships, and was a finalist in the Eastern United States Championships in both the Professional Open American Smooth and Professional Open International Latin Divisions. Jeff's greatest pride is the more than thirty top teacher awards he has won and having kept his position consistently in the list of the top 75 teachers in North America. This was done while competing professionally and performing an average of more then one show per week.

Jeff holds associate credentials with the Imperial Society of Teachers of Dance and the Pan American Teachers Association. In addition to this text, *Quickstart to Social Dancing*, Jeff is completing the second of eleven books in the Quickstart Series, (*Quickstart To Tango* is scheduled to be released in December, 1997). Jeff continues to offer the highest standard in teaching beginners and advanced students including teachers and professional performers.

An Important Note to the Reader

Maximum benefit will be achieved if the user of this book reads the entire text before beginning his lessons. In this way will you best be mentally prepared to begin. The special lay-flat binding will keep the pages from flipping and increase the life expectancy of the book. The student will observe the logical and cumulative flow of the lesson structure and presentation. The actual text can be read in one or two hours. The text and diagrams have been designed for easy visual and physical use. The book is a shortcut in itself. Please do not try to skip around or start at the end. I know this will be a great temptation, but please resist the urge.

A third person can participate by reading the verbal directions for the one or more couples taking the lesson. In this way you will hear my words and simply follow my directions. Please remember all dance steps begin on the first beat of music.

Mr. Allen is available to answer any of your questions regarding this book. His readers may contact him through the QQS website:

http://home.earthlink.net/~dancebook/

or email directly to:

dancebook@earthlink.net

Thank you for purchasing *Quickstart to Social Dancing* and please enjoy yourselves.

Acknowledgments

To Whitney,

A man may only be entitled to one miracle in his lifetime, if this is the case, I have had more than my portion. You are my miracle! My saying, "Life has indeed been hard these last several years," would be the height of under-statement. There have been times when it seemed it would be better if the Earth itself would swallow me. Then there was you, at the edge of the dark pit, to snatch me up and out to the solid ground. Right now, my love, it seems if you look closely the Sun is trying to make its appearance. 6/19/96

To my children—Joshua, Bethanie, & Jessica,

You three are extraordinarily talented and beautiful. It is a blessing to be your Dad. I know that your lives will be enriched even as you have and continue to enrich mine.

To all of my past and especially my present students,

Without you, I would have nothing to teach nor would I know what I could teach. I am deeply indebted to you all!

The index of this text has been prepared by Whitney A. Brown.

Warning/Disclaimer

This book is designed to provide information in regard to the subject matter covered. It is sold with the understanding that neither the publisher nor the author intends the reader to engage in any physical activity that can be construed as out of the ordinary. There is no intent by the publisher and author to cause the reader to unduly exert or strain himself physically. Each movement covered by this text is considered by the publisher and author to be well within the realm of ordinary and normal movement for a healthy human. A healthy human being has no physical problems concerning motor skills, or the use of joints or muscles. Should you experience pain from any movement in general or upon beginning to use this text, you should seek the advice of your physician before continuing. Do not exceed any limitations of movement your physician suggests.

This book is designed to provide the most basic and simple dance lessons and dance level experience. *Quickstart to Social Dancing* is the very beginning of your partner dancing experience. It is very suitable for those who just want to get by. Anyone who expects to dance very well must be prepared to invest a lot of time and money.

Every effort has been made to make this manual as complete within its scope and as accurate as possible. However, there may be mistakes, both typographical and in content. Therefore, this text should be used only as a general guide and not as the ultimate source of dance information.

The purpose of this text is to educate and entertain. The author and QQS Publications have neither liability nor responsibility to any person or entity with respect to any loss or damage caused, or alleged to be caused, directly or indirectly by the information contained in this book.

If you do not wish to be bound by the above, you may return this book to the publisher, in marketable condition, for a full refund. (Please include your cash register receipt).

Contents

Introduction

Social partner dancing is a means of recreation and enjoyment for a lifetime. There are no sociological, chronological, or economic boundaries in social dancing. When you are out for the evening dancing with your partner—you are spending your time wisely. Anyone would be hard pressed to find another activity the basis of which depends on the synchronized physical and mental cooperation of a man and a woman so much as social dancing does. Social Dancing requires this togetherness and rewards us with so much more. Dancing has always and will always satisfy the emotional, the artistic, the intellectual, the physical, and yes even the competitive spirit of its participants.

Once you begin using, *Quickstart to Social Dancing*, you will find learning to dance using my very simple method will be fun and definitely intoxicating. You will experience the need to go past the contents of this book. However, we have a job to do together and that special event is just around the corner. Is it a wedding or a New Year's Eve party? The type of special event you're attending really makes no difference; this time you and your partner are really going to enjoy yourselves. Maybe you'll be the one couple that everyone talks about when the last note of music has been played. Don't laugh; it could happen!

I have written this book in a form that I believe is as simple as possible for you the reader—

my new student.

Quickstart to Social Dancing, is presented as if you were my private student taking individual instruction by yourself or with your partner.

I will be talking to you and telling you exactly what to do moment by moment.

I have made your instruction as easy as walking, talking, and feeling.

These are physical attributes that you already possess; therefore, learning to dance will be easy.

Basically, you will repeat aloud what I tell you to say, and then follow your own simple commands.

There will be nothing to figure out or interpret. Exactly what you need to know to begin dancing for that special event is included in this book. Only a minute segment of our population has really taken dance lessons beyond the level of this book. Believe me, the experts are very few and far between and they have been there. The intimidation only exists within you. Just go out there and expect to really enjoy yourselves.

We will spend much time with repetition and yet you will learn at a very fast pace. You can learn one dance or all six of them. It makes no difference. The first dance you will learn will prepare you to get right out there on the Social Dance floor.

You will learn at your own pace and comfort level. Each lesson in this book will become easier because of the cumulative building block method I have presented.

Once you have learned to take a lesson successfully, use this technique over and over for each new lesson.

The very first lesson will simply teach you to walk better. What could be easier than that? Walking is a skill you already possess. We will simply teach you to understand more about it and to use it rhythmically. Do not be afraid of the word rhythm. Believe it or not you already have rhythm. Rhythm is demonstrated when you repeat any physical skill that is currently within your command.

I will teach you to unlock the rhythm you already possess with the friendly use of your own voice and your present walking skills.

Then we will learn to make friends with rhythm and use it coincidentally with music.

I wrote *Quickstart to Social Dancing*, using the "KISS" rule; that is "Keep It Simple, Stupid." I wrote this book because until now there have "charts" and "pictures of footprints on the floor" for do-it-yourself people and beginners. Many people, including those that already teach social dancing, find the charts very difficult to understand. Because it takes so long to understand and execute the chart form of dance instruction even fledgling or inexperienced teachers shy away from them. The basic flaw with the charts is that you do not fully comprehend them until you can execute the figure with theoretic perfection. Pictures of footprints become visually confusing because they try to show too much at once. The footprints do not relate to the three dimensionality of dancing.

Over a period of 15 years I have taught thousands of people to dance with a partner. I have come to understand that the more senses you encourage the student to use, the quicker the student learns. The key to successful dance instruction for both men and women is to take what they already know how to do and improve on it. My feeling is that if the reader can negotiate a staircase both upwards and downwards with no railing, then this book will be simple to use. Furthermore you should enjoy a lifetime of Social Partner Dancing.

Now it is time to get down to business! Please remember to treat yourself and your partner kindly!

Understanding What Constitutes a Dance Step

A body weight change from one foot to the next is what really completes a dance step.

This means you must move your body until you have attained a new vertical position with all your weight over the next foot. (You will not learn to dance successfully by just putting your feet towards some designated location. This is an old method of teaching dance that your brain does not relate to within its already established program for movement).

Your brain is much happier if you learn to place or move your body to a designated location. In this way your legs and feet accommodate the movement of your body every single time. An example of this would be to pick up an object from one point in the room and place it at another point in the room. Absolutely no thoughts were given about your legs or feet when doing this. Over the years of my teaching I have had the opportunity to witness very intelligent and successful people stymied in their attempts to learn to dance when exposed to the old method. They have tried just learning choreographed patterns known as footsteps or figures, without the understanding of a directional body weight change.

Contact points of the feet should be felt through the shoe as if you are barefoot on the dance floor.

A better idea is to think of your feet as empty glasses and your body as a pitcher of water. You complete a dance step in the same way you fill the glass with water. The pitcher is lifted from one location and brought to a position that is suspended over the glass. The water contained in the pitcher is freely and unrestrictedly poured into the glass until the glass is filled. Likewise, your body is lifted from one location toward another location.

Your body is suspended over that location just long enough to load up the horizontal platform known as your foot. The first location from which the body was lifted is known as your supporting or standing leg and foot. This supporting leg and foot supply the energy to move your body's mass to the next leg and foot. In the case of the pitcher, your hand and arm supplied this energy.

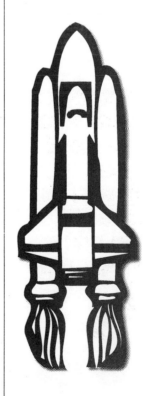

Another example that you may relate to is the action and reaction of a rocket ship blasting off a launching pad. The weight and pressure from the body's force propel the body away from the dance floor and the supporting foot. Some of you know this to be Newton's Third Law, plus the factors that relate to the acceleration of mass. The important thing to remember is a dance step is only complete when your body has traveled from one platform to the next. Those platforms are, of course, your feet.

What We Measure When We Say Timing...

Another reason the old foot placement method hinders many people from learning to dance is that they do not gain an appreciation of the time the body takes to travel to the next leg and foot. You often hear these sorry folks complain about having no rhythm, despite the fact that every repetitive physical skill they currently execute requires rhythm. In the case of the pitcher, water, and glass scenario, it took time to pour the water into the glass.

TIME TIME TIME

Several physical events took place in sequence, which could not have occurred all at the same time. The time expended to lift the body from the first platform or supporting leg and then suspend the body in flight long enough to fill the next platform or foot is what we must measure.

- This measured time is equal to the beat structure or timing of the music to which you will be dancing. This beat structure or rhythm of the music will be counted in increments of Quick counts or Slow counts. You will be learning to effectively use this Quick and Slow method of counting throughout *Quickstart to Social Dancing*.

- This is a summary of how and what you will learn from the Quickstart Program.

- Each footstep or dance step you will take will require a timed body weight change to be a successfully completed dance step. You will become physically comfortable with moving forward, backward, and sideways with a partner.

- You will also learn to distinguish one dance characteristic and type from another and apply them to the proper music.

- We will do this for six dances: FOXTROT, WALTZ, RUMBA, MERENGUE, SWING, and CHA-CHA.

In just three to four hours you and your partner should be able to take the lessons learned in *Quickstart to Social Dancing*, right out to the Social Dance floor. You should be able to do one, two, or maybe three of the dances with which you have worked. *Quickstart to Social Dancing*, is especially useful if you have a special occasion such as a wedding coming up. It will be perfect for those who are going on a resort vacation or on a cruise. Give yourself a special anniversary, birthday, or Valentine's Day present. Prepare a day or two in advance, and go out dancing that weekend. Have a ball!

Some Things To Do Before We Begin...

Please note: Attempt the following only if this is part of your normal activity and you do this on a regular basis. If you normally need the use of a handrail when traveling a staircase, do not do the following! You do not need to follow this particular illustration or direction to learn to dance.

Traveling The Staircase

I want you to travel up and down a staircase several times without the use of a handrail. I want you to pay particular attention to the automatic control and search for balance your body and brain provide you. You will find the focus of this automatic support system is centered on your tummy and ribcage.

For most people the structuring of their body while ascending or descending a staircase is superior to their usual body position. This is very important. The structure of your and your partner's bodies must be controlled in a like manner.

- We try to bring balance to the dance partnership rather than search for it from our partner in the same way we search for a handrail on a staircase. Basically, we want to create a dance couple that is one unit, not two individuals. Remember your body, arms and head are supported by your own legs.

- To do so your ribcage and tummy must be in control at all times. We cannot have your bodies floundering around moving in random directions now can we?

- The height of the staircase instantly became your motivation for balance. Your ribcage and shoulders remained parallel to the stair treads while you were moving. Your ribcage was also parallel to your hip and pelvis assemblies.

- Throughout your Social Dance lessons and social dancing think of your ribs as one railroad track. The parallel line level with the floor formed from the left to right pelvis must be thought of as the other track. These tracks must remain parallel as they travel around your body.

- Your ribcage must experience lift on each and every dance step. An experienced dancer will flex each and every muscle surrounding and immediately below the ribcage. This muscular flex includes both the front and back of the ribcage. I cannot stress the importance of making this a good habit from the beginning of your dance experience!

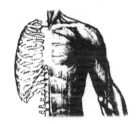

**Your
ribcage must
experience
lift with each
dance step.**

The Music You Will Need

You need to have some music. Any good record or tape store, new or used, will have some generic ballroom dance music. I recommend the CD format. Check the international music section in the store if they do not have a section for Social Dancing. Take a list of song titles to the store with you that may have been recommended by an acquaintance or found at the end of this text. We are going to learn Foxtrot, Waltz, Rumba, Merengue, Swing and Cha-Cha, so your music must include all the dances we are going to learn. There are clear prompts to the correct cut on the CD and that repeat function is just wonderful for practice.

PLEASE SEE:

**Suggested
Music for
Dancing at
the back of
this book.**

Some Space To Dance

Once you have chosen a place to begin our little lesson together you must clear enough space to dance. The area needed to execute "The Quickstart," program is about the size of your Dining Room Table. Five feet by eight feet will be fine. Do not forget, you had to have room around the table for your dining room chairs.

- A hardwood floor is best.

- A tile floor is the next best choice, and hopefully, it is not over concrete. That makes a very hard surface and is tough on your feet, ankles, and knees. This is especially the case over prolonged periods of time. Practice in your sneakers if this is the case. A low piled carpet, you know the indoor/outdoor or commercial type will do fine. Practice in your socks if you're going to "Cut a Rug."

- If it is nice outside, put your sneakers on and take your dance lesson out on the patio or even your driveway. Make sure you block the entrance to the driveway.

- If you live in an apartment complex it may have a recreation room or small gym that you can use. If there are mirrors available so much the better. Mirrors are a wonderful aid to learning. You will be able to see just how wonderful you look TOGETHER. Get your boom box and some of your friends and neighbors, and have a party.

OK...Now We Are Ready to Learn the Quickstart to Social Dancing Program.

LESSON ONE:
The Linear Directions of the Dance Couple.

The first thing we must learn to do is walk together in a straight line.

To do this I want both of you to stand next to each other in a side by side position. We must practice accurate directional movement. Hopefully one of you was either a Boy Scout or Girl Scout at some point in your lifetime. You are going to make your bodies a living compass.

Your nose and your belly button will always face the same direction. Your legs when placed on a compass heading will become the needle of that compass.

I want the gentleman to place all of his weight on the Right Foot leaving the Left Foot free of weight. I want the Woman to place all of her weight on the Left Foot leaving the Right Foot free. We will always start in this manner throughout the Quickstart Program— once you have begun the dance figure section. **Just in case you have forgotten, your starting dance position will be the left foot free for the man, and right foot free for the woman.**

The first compass heading is due north. With your body absolutely parallel to a wall in your new little dance studio, due north is determined by creating two geometric lines.

The first line would be vertical from your nose to your belly button through to the floor. This first line makes you absolutely straight up and down throughout your body.

The second line begins where the first line meets the dance floor. This second line is perpendicular from the plane of your body to the wall. The plane of your body would be where you would divide the front of the hip assembly from the back as if you split the body vertically into two parts. Imagine stretching a tightrope between your body and the wall. You must walk on the imaginary tightrope as your new line of dance. To be a good partner and a successful dancer, when you walk either forward or backward I want you to attempt to be this accurate. Never actually use a tightrope!

Now I want both of you to walk four steps forward due north, more if you have room, in exactly the same cadence or speed.

Accuracy in the directional movement of your body is the key to good partnering skills. Please do not take this section lightly.

As you begin to walk forward you will please notice that your knees flex slightly. Every single movement of your body will definitely include a slight flex in the knee. This flex will occur regardless of the directions of forwards, backwards, or sideways that the dance couple will travel.

Walking forward also included another very ordinary occurrence. The bottom of the heel of your shoe struck the floor first.

This place of contact on the lady's flat or gentleman's shoe is approximately ½ inch from the back edge of the heel of the shoe. Do not attempt to walk on the very back edge of the heel where the flat of the heel meets the rise of the heel. There is no support for the body on this edge. You must feel your natural heel.

Learning to walk forward in the Foxtrot and the Waltz will include the use of this natural heel placement first. I will direct you otherwise when a different foot placement is required. Until then, just walk normally.

JEFF SAYS:

"Always feel compression of muscle when the knees flex— no sitting on the job allowed. Feel a light release when your knees straighten for smooth motion."

A Quick and a Slow
Word About Timing...

The cadence or count I referred to previously will be: 1,2 for the first step; 3,4 for the second step; 5,6 for the third step; and 7,8 for the fourth step.

- By the way, from now on while studying *Quickstart to Social Dancing*, **a movement of 2 increments or beats of music will be called a SLOW.** This cadence of a slow count in this lesson will always take two increments or beats of music regardless of our directional path.

- The two beats of music will represent the total time it takes to walk, move, or change weight from one foot to the next. I want to remind you once again we will call this cadence a SLOW.

- When dancing we can also walk, move, or change weight from one foot to the next in one beat of music or increment of time. We will call this one beat of music a QUICK. **A SLOW takes exactly twice the time duration of a QUICK.** A quick takes exactly one half the time duration of that of a slow count. The important point to remember is the proportional relationship between a Slow count and a Quick count of time.

- It is just like shoveling sand. One shovel full and its discharge is a quick. Two shovels full with their discharge would be a slow. This is very important! When you begin the Dance Steps, or call them Dance Figures if you will, we will always use the terminology of quicks and slows for counting the music.

- It will be much easier for you to count with Quicks & Slows and right now we want everything to be easy. As you practice your walking steps please count aloud to the tempo I have instructed you to use. For instance, four walking steps would be counted aloud as "Slow-Slow-Slow-Slow". Do this and you will learn quickly how to get into the music and make it your friend. The Four Slows equal the 8 count cadence.

You can walk backwards as if you were blindfolded.

Now I want both of you to repeat this walking procedure backwards which would be due south. Make sure both of you retain the same cadence counting aloud, and please do not fall off your imaginary tightrope! Your count for the backwards walks will be "Slow- Slow- Slow- Slow."

- I want to give you a little hint about walking backwards. OK, it is a big hint. Since you cannot turn your head around and look where you are going, you are indeed blind when traveling backwards.

- Just one moment prior to moving your body backward, lightly and swiftly swing your thigh backward so that the big toe of your foot touches the floor behind you.

- The swing of your leg in a light and swift manner should never cause movement or sway in your upper body.

- In this way you will be like a blind man with his cane. Knowing that you are in contact with the dance floor is a confidence builder, so you can proceed without too much caution. Even if you were to bang into anything, including the wall behind you, it would only be with the bottom of your foot. You do not have to bang the wall to test this point!

This will not cause damage to anyone or anything because the leg is quite loose at this point. When you put your weight on the foot naturally you apply much more pressure than this.

The accurate placement of your feet and your continued counting aloud using this cadence of slows is increasing your learning curve.

I have been able to determine that this speed in learning is increased by at least seven times. This comparison is based on those who take dance lessons without concentrating on qualitative movement and timing.

Always count aloud when taking a lesson or practicing.

Sideways is the Third
and Last Linear Direction

Now we are going to work on side steps and closing the feet with a weight change. **The action of moving the foot to the side and then following that action with closing the free foot to it is commonly called a Chassé in dancing.** It is a French word that means chase. The idea here is that the foot moving to the side is chased by the closing foot. We will use the Chassé as a predominant dance step in three of the upcoming dances: Merengue, Swing and Cha-Cha. I will remind you of this as it happens so you can refer back to this section.

You may not know it, but we are getting very close to success!

- I want the gentleman and the lady to face each other with your bodies parallel to each other. Sorry, no contact yet, but you will be in contact very soon.

- You should be on the proper standing foot and each partner should have the correct free foot available for its swing action to the side.

REMEMBER:

**Slightly Flex
Your Knees**

• Remember, to begin any action that includes movement of the body in partner dancing, a very slight flex of the knee is necessary. This flex brings you or your partner into the music and keeps you from looking like a robot.

• You will also notice that as a result of bending your knee while swinging your leg, the first part of the foot that touched the floor is the inside edge of the foot. Important: Side Steps are from six to eighteen inches wide; no more, no less.

• This use of the inside edge of the foot helps create a smooth soft action which can not be attained if the whole sole of the foot is placed down at once. This type of foot action is very important!

• Try both ways and you will see and feel the difference. This technique will be particularly beneficial for the Latin rhythms we will learn.

Side Steps and Closes Travel Faster.

At this beginner level of partner dancing your side steps are generally quicker than your forward or backward steps. Use this quicker idea to relate to the timing of quick-quick. we already discussed that a quick will take just one beat of music.

- I want you to begin moving to the side about eight to ten inches wide and to the cadence of 1-2-3-4-5-6-7-8.

- This equals a total of 8 quicks, and don't forget to count aloud.

- Please move Side, Together-Side, Together-Side, Together-Side, Together. Remember: average eight to ten inches wide. Are you ready? Go!

- Closing the feet in social dancing and forgetting to change your body weight to the closing foot is definitely the most common error in any type of social partner dancing.

**Closing the
Feet is So
Easy—
We Forget
Why We
Did It.**

We always change weight automatically when the body travels from one location to another. Our brain instinctively senses the need to move the body to the next foot when the body starts to travel.

- This is part of the software that we were programmed with from birth. All you have to do is watch a baby learning to walk to realize this is true. When the baby's parents call the baby, the child attempts to move from one foot to the next. No one can possibly teach the baby to do that!

- The brain, however, senses no need at all to change weight to a foot that is swinging to an ending position under our body but is not causing any bodyflight or movement. Therefore there is no instinctive need to put the body weight on the closing foot.

- The beginner must use an intellectual command to cause the body weight to change to that foot. The beginner must really concentrate on this Closing Step in all the dance figures we learn in the Quickstart to Social Dance Program.

- Lack of weight change while using the closing step will certainly be the point where you will step on your partner's foot. We certainly do not want that to happen. The required body weight change on the closing step will soon become instinctive and without hesitation to your dancing as you follow my advice in the next section.

JEFF SAYS:

"At this early stage of learning dance, the mastery of the Closing Action, or Step, will provide many happy hours in your social dance calendar."

Pay Particular Attention to the Together or What is Known as a Close or Closing Step.

- In order to maintain an alternating use of the feet: Left-Right-Left-Right, etc., you had to instantly release the foot that was on the floor supporting the body. Lift this supporting foot no more than one half inch.

- The reason for this is that the weight had to be transferred to the foot that was closing from the foot that was supporting the body. This is extremely important!

- **From now on whenever you close either foot to the other foot this counts as a weight change, and you must instantly release that standing or supporting foot from the floor.**

- When you instantly release your supporting foot from the floor you must use your knee and thigh to lift that foot no more than $1/2$ inch. Do not use your shoulders to change your body weight from one foot to another and you will never look like a robot.

" You don't want to look like me!"

23

Relax! It is good food for the muscles.

You probably think all of this seems quite simple. Well, that is terrific! As long as you keep that great attitude, you will be feeding all the muscles in your body very positive information.

- Remember that all muscle usage begins with electrical impulses deep in the brain's central nervous system.

- A chemical known as ATP (Adenosine Triphosphate) is released to the muscles. It acts like a food or vitamin. When you get tense it burns the food. Burnt food is too crisp, hard, and overdone. The ATP is supercharged with heat and will cause the joints operated by certain muscle groups to stiffen and react differently than you planned.

- Your muscles will not perform anywhere near their capability. In other physical activities and sports athletes refer to this as "CHOKING." Once stress or anger has invaded your practice time, stop! The stress will cause you to be totally counterproductive.

- You must treat yourself and your partner kindly. **Eliminate all negative emotion from your learning and practice time.** I certainly want you to have a lot of fun while you are learning to dance.

Practice for Success — the REVIEW

- We have learned that when dancing you must move your bodies in very accurate linear directions. North is forward from your center. South is backward from your center. Both North and South are perpendicular tangents related to the plane of your body.

- The plane of your body is a straight line that passes through shoulder-to-shoulder and/or hip-to-hip. A side step or a closing step moves either east or west on a line directly under the plane of the hips. We have learned that a slow is two beats of music and that a quick is one beat of music.

- So far all your forward or backward walking was done with a Slow count. Later on we will introduce them as also being done with a Quick count. All of the sidesteps and closing steps you take will remain as a Quick count. The average sidestep is eight to ten inches wide.

- Do not forget to take the standing foot off the dance floor $\frac{1}{2}$ inch immediately after you have closed the free or moving foot.

- You should feel you are simply improving the quality of your walking as a result of these suggestions and techniques. Congratulations. In dancing you must move with a higher quality carriage, known as Dance Poise, than you typically use when you walk.

- The KEY to good dancing will be to maintain your Dance Poise while being connected to your dance partner.

- Believe it or not, many people who partner dance in any of the various forms, have never learned this. No matter how many steps or patterns they do, they still look very sloppy and their reciprocity with their partner is poor. My students, after having learned this, all look and feel good. You are included!

- Now practice the previous lesson side by side and also in front of each other with music. This practice is done without physical contact.

- For your selection of music please choose a Foxtrot, the most popular smooth dance in the world. Doing this to the music for about a half hour will bring you to the end of this phase or Lesson # 1 of the Quickstart to Social Dancing program.

- Do not attempt to go beyond this point until you can move with qualitative poise in time with the music. Refer to the seemingly simple directions above. They are really power packed with information. These directions may seem a bit boring but they are definitely the key to good partner dancing. If you are not able to move in time and in stride with your partner while maintaining timing with the music, you are not really dancing are you?

LESSON TWO:
Embracing Your Partner...
Now the Fun Really Begins!

We have to discuss a little about the dance frame that makes up the single entity known as a dance couple. I must quickly dispel any idea or notion that moving in as a couple with the quality poise you have developed from the previous lesson; you will step on your partner's feet. Every single person that has walked out onto a dance floor has feared this social faux pas. This fear has actually prevented many faint hearted souls from ever participating in any form of social partner dancing. The memory of such an incident has stopped others from returning to the dance floor. There is no need to fear. We have a very special way of embracing each other that allows us to move together as ONE.

Have No Fear, The Toes Will Disappear!

The Partner's Dance Position and Frame

This section will teach you how to line up with your partner and you will use this exact lineup when we teach you the embrace.

- I know you realize from our development of improved rhythmic walking skills in correct geometric tangents there is a potential to step on your partner's toes. This is because you are standing directly in line with each other, nose to nose and toes to toes.

- I agree with this concern and we must now teach you a new body to body alignment. After you have learned to use this new alignment, a closed embrace with your partner will never contain the jeopardy of stepping on their foot when walking forward.

- What I want you to know is the foot you are most likely to step on is not the one you would expect! Most of us would expect to step on the foot in front of us, but this is not the case.

- A natural phenomenon that occurs from the swing of our pelvis is called Body Swing. With the action of Body Swing our left leg and foot will swing forward and make contact with the left leg and foot of our partner. Remember that theoretic or invisible tightrope you learned to walk on. It is directly under the center of your body between, not in front of, your feet. Therefore your left foot, when used correctly, has a natural propensity to swing slightly rightwards. The reverse application would also be true.

- So what just one of you must do is move to your left just enough so the point of the right shoe is on the line that would be your partner's tightrope. Now I want you to maintain a space between your feet and your partner's feet, with toes facing each other's, of no less than 4 inches and no more than six inches.

- If you have done this correctly, your bodies will line up as follows:

  1st—The right foot of each partner is dead between the partner's feet or to use my analogy on the partner's tightrope.

  2nd—The vertical center of the right thigh of each partner is directly opposite each other.

  3rd—The right side of the gentleman's rib cage is opposite the sternum or vertical center of the lady's rib cage.

JEFF SAYS:

"Moving with someone attached to us is not natural. Therefore, everyone must learn to do it. We are not born with a natural skill to PARTNER someone else."

4th—The right side of the woman's rib cage is approximately opposite the gentleman's sternum. Two partners would have to be exactly the same size for these reference points to be perfect, and that is unlikely.

5th—The chin of the gentleman is in line with or pointing over the woman's right shoulder.

6th—The chin of the woman is in line with or pointing towards the gentleman's right shoulder.

Again, the approximate rule must apply, so please do not squabble over these dimensions. I am sorry ladies; if there is a big height disparity between you and your partner, your view will be obstructed. Now, with both partners in line, we will learn to take what is known as the partner's dance hold or dance position. **So long as you move to the same cadence and remain in line with your bodies, the toes you may have thought were there, have disappeared.**

When you take each other in your arms, use the exact lineup you learned a few moments ago.

We Are Going to Learn Use and Position of Our Arms Now.

- The first item to remember is the shoulders are always relaxed and positioned down towards the rib cage.

- The muscles around the front and back of the rib cage will flex and provide a shelf for the arms rather than your trying to sustain the necessary lift in the upper arms with the shoulders.

The reason I told you this first is 999 out of 1,000 people when told to lift their arms into dance position will use the top of their shoulders like a shrug. This is wrong and can cause painful cramping if allowed to persist. It is for this reason that people produce such a poor dance frame. They are instinctively avoiding this pain in the shoulders.

Now you know what not to do. Here is the correct procedure to lift and maintain the dance position.

- With both your elbows pointing 45 degrees at the dance floor relax your underarms and push the upper arms up by flexing all the muscles that surround the front, side, and back of your rib cage. I bet you would never have thought of that!

- It may also be helpful to think of lifting a large tray with the Thanksgiving turkey on it for all to see. The inside of your arm at the elbows is inclined toward the ceiling. You should find this to be easy and relaxed, providing you with the ability to sustain the position comfortably for several minutes at a time.

- Using this process to lift your upper arms, bring them to the level of your bust line or sternum. Check to see if you can swing your forearms from your elbows like a windshield wiper without dropping the elbows or the upper arms.

- I want the lady to give the gentleman her right hand by placing the base of her palm (the area just above the wrist) into the center of his palm. This way as she closes the fingers gently the lady's fingers will reach over to the back of his left hand. This handhold is comfortable and when he gets nervous or thinks intensely the lady's fingers cannot be squeezed to the point of turning purple.

• Gentlemen, with the middle finger of your right hand, touch the lady's back just below her shoulder blade. Do this without compromising your upper arm position. The triangle formed between the neck and each shoulder, and from elbow to elbow, should resemble a coat hanger.

The lady will place her left hand on the gentleman's upper arm without reaching or compromising her arm position. The lady's left hand generally comes to rest just below the gentleman's shoulder cap (between the biceps and the deltoid). The joined hands are held at the level of the lady's eye line. Congratulations, you have now become the single entity known as a dance couple!

This is the end of Lesson 2 in the Quickstart to Social Dancing Program.

LESSON THREE:
Learning to Move Together is a Lot of Fun. Keep It That Way!

- As you begin the following section there are some important ideas of expression I want you to keep in mind.

- Regardless of which member of the dance couple is traveling backwards the space they provide by doing so is a form of invitation.

- That invitation says, "Come through the point where I was to meet me." That invitation is accepted willingly and aggressively.

- This provides the feeling and emotion of togetherness and oneness.

- The movement through the partner's space will be the acceptance of the invitation.

- This will be welcome and effective in creating a good look and quality dancing, as long as the dance couple maintains their arm frame and the lineup.

Before we charge ahead with the selection of dance figures and dance rhythms I have in store for you, we must repeat all of the moving exercises we developed in Lesson 1.

• Make sure you count aloud for each other in order to bring yourselves into the Music. Please remember that to begin any movement the knees must flex slightly. This will make sure your entire bodies begin to move as you commence to dance. The lady is also alerted by this flexing action as to when the gentleman is about to begin. Make no mistake about it, this movement together with the controlled cadence of the music IS dancing. Please count aloud to insure your moving harmoniously and in a synchronized fashion with your partner.

Always count aloud for each other when practicing or taking a lesson.

- The quality that you produce now with these simple movement exercises will be taken by you into the development of your dance choreography. Please stay on your tightrope. Look ahead; do not look at the floor.

- Pick points in the room at your eye level to move towards or away from. People move 100 times better with their heads up if for no other reason than they can see were they are going.

You saw your feet this morning at the end of your bed when you woke up and when you put on your socks and shoes. There is no need to see them again. Remember, the toes of your partner have disappeared.

When you have practiced this moving exercise enough to make it reasonably smooth with the music you have completed Lesson 3 in the Quickstart to Social Dancing Program. Yeah!

Remember we have several objectives in using The Quickstart to Social Dancing Program. The first objective is to get you out on the dance floor. This will happen as fast as possible and keep you looking as good as possible.

- The six dance rhythms you will learn will keep you out on the dance floor all night long.

- The previous lessons have produced quality in your movement.

- The lessons have also taught you to move to a cadence.

Any top flight professional dancer will tell you that timing and balance are everything to the dance couple. **A dance couple elegantly doing only one or two dance figures per dance rhythm is always preferable to one doing a sloppy mess of many uncontrolled dance steps.**

I know you have heard the expression, "A jack of all trades, a master of none." I do not want this to be you. You will master one or two dance figures per dance, and you will learn to turn them. Therefore, your concentration will be focused on the wonderful music you will dance to with your delightful partner.

Both of you will look beautiful together. There is definitely something unique about a dance couple that makes them look better than they ever could alone! You will be that one couple at the wedding, Christmas party or fund-raiser that looks as if they know what they are doing and are having a wonderful time doing it!

The Important Attributes of Choreography or Dance Steps

You have already done the hard part! The peak of the mountain is now in sight.

The choreography—the Dance Figures—begin!

What are the important attributes?

The directions we will use when partnering each other will be from the gentleman's body. The lady will proceed in the natural opposite direction. I am truly sorry ladies, but the man leads in social dancing. He must get a chance once in a while to do that!

As I told you earlier in place of numeric counting we will use all Quicks and Slows. You should count aloud for your partner. This makes the music more user friendly.

The beginning of Lesson 4 in the Quickstart to Social Dancing Program.

The Important
Attributes of
Choreography
or Your
Dance
Steps

Counting aloud during practice brings the familiar and friendly sound of your own voice into coincidence with the music. Hearing the music and your voice at the same time is a great device for getting right into the music rather than waiting to hear the music and then trying to begin. If you use the wait and begin method, by the time you hear the starting point you are already late. Music has an unforgiving nature in that it is continuous and consistent. Internalizing the sound of the music in the same way we can internalize the sound of our voice will give us the musical and rhythmic feeling. Overlapping this feeling with your hearing of the music will soon become automatic. At this point you will no longer have to count aloud. **The only shortcut to developing this skill is to compress the time by the frequency and repetition of what I have suggested.**

Your voice and the musical sound are energy. Foot pressure derived from your body weight on the dance floor is energy. When you put the two of these energy sources together, **sound and foot pressure**, they will quickly **link the music to your balance and movement** from one foot to the next. I cannot stress enough the importance of the previous statement!

Remember foot pressure is generated only when your body is vertically aligned in a position over your foot. This is a dance step! Some poor folks believe that the simple act of putting your foot somewhere per directional instructions will do the trick. That type of foot action is merely a tap or touch, not a dance step. These sometimes argumentative folks are never going to learn. Why? Once again, **dancing takes the use of full body weight over the foot to match the force found in the sound of music.**

I call these pitiful students argumentative because over and over they delude themselves into believing if they, "Only knew where to put their feet they would get it." They fight the natural usage of their body that is the leg and foot following the direction the body intends to move toward, and they fight good counsel from a qualified and very experienced instructor.

To simply prove my case ask your partner to go and pick up something in the room. Watch to see that their body turns to face the object and then inclines toward that object as the body projects from the supporting foot. They begin to move, and the legs and feet follow. At no time during this little experiment did their feet lurch ahead of the body because the body was moving!

For one moment please visualize the beach or a swimming pool. What do you do when testing the water temperature? Why of course, you dip or tap your foot into the water and at that moment have no inclination to move forward into the water. The act of **tapping your foot** out to the water **produces a** stiffening or **holding** action in your body **preventing movement**. Similar placement of your foot will never produce movement on the dance floor.

That pathetic student is still arguing with the Laws of Physics, themselves, and by this time everyone around them. They are obstinate and by this time very frustrated with their negative learning curve. They may try one or two more lessons and then quit. They will tell somebody else they just cannot seem to get it or that they did not like the class or the teacher. Simply stated, they used the wrong body tools and approach to dancing. Please, please, please do not join them in their obstinacy and failure.

OK, my editorial is finished and I have your attention. We are going to use exactly the same skills learned in your prior lessons to develop your social dancing skills with your partner.

LESSON FOUR:
The BOX STEP is Your
Pathfinder and Trailblazer.

1. Start out side by side. This will only take a couple of minutes. After we are done with this little exercise we will place you in the above described Dance Frame and related body positions and you will be dancing!

2. We will call this section the **Forward Half Box**. It does not have a gender. Both Partners will always do the Forward Half Box using the following method.

3. **Repeat Aloud:** "My body moves forward." Now do it. Yes, both of you will participate in this way. Move away from your right foot and finish on top of your left. Your right foot is now free of any body weight and therefore it has to be the next foot!

4. **Repeat Aloud:** "My body moves sideways." Now do it. Your body moves away from your left foot and finishes on top of your right foot. Average stepping about twelve wide for these sidesteps. Your left foot is free of any body weight and therefore the left foot has to be next!

5. **Repeat Aloud:** "Now I close my feet." Please close the left foot to the right foot until the heel of each foot is $\frac{1}{4}$ inch apart from each other. Then instantly take the right foot off the floor no more than $\frac{1}{2}$ inch. Your right foot is now free of all body weight and therefore is the next foot. Do you see how simple this is? My words repeat themselves, you repeat the words, and then are empowered to move dynamically and confidently. This completes the Forward Half Box step.

Something Important You Must Remember

I trust you remember the previous lesson about closes of the feet and how important they are? If not, please take a moment and review that portion of this book. One of the main keys to the success of the Quickstart to Social Dancing Program is the Closing Step! It is the common denominator to every single figure we will do. It occurs every single time, so please perfect it. Now let us return to our Box Step lesson. We are half done with learning the Full Box Step.

We are now going to learn the Backward Half Box. Again I will remind you that the Backward Half Box is gender free and we will refer to either the Backward Half Box or the Forward Half Box frequently. They will be done by either the gentleman or the lady as the choreography calls for them to be done.

6. **Repeat Aloud:** "My body moves backwards."
Now it is your turn to actually do it. Your body moves
away from the left foot until it is over the right foot. Your
left foot is free of body weight and therefore is the next
foot that will move.

You have to remember the blind man illustration in the
former lesson about walking backwards. It is another
key to smooth, effortless, and trouble free social
dancing. You may want to review that small section of
Quickstart to Social Dancing at this time.

7. **Repeat Aloud:** "My body moves sideways."
Now it is your turn to do it. Your body moves away
from your supporting foot, that is your right foot, until
the weight of your body is completely over the left foot.
Average stepping about twelve to the side.

8. **Repeat Aloud:** "Now I close my feet."
Close the right foot to your left foot until the heels are
$\frac{1}{4}$ inch apart from each other and take your left foot off
the floor no more than $\frac{1}{2}$ inch. Your left foot is now free
of all body weight and therefore is the next foot.

CONGRATULATIONS, you have just completed both the
Forward Half Box and the Backward Half Box. When
these two figures are done together, they comprise the
foundation and the most fundamental dance figure done
in social dancing.

This figure known generically as the Dancer's Square Step or the Box Step will be the basis for our, Quickstart to Social Dancing Program. From the Dancer's Square Step or the Box Step we will build your ability to use this basic pattern comprised of only three directions into 6 major dances and dance rhythms.

I want my readers to know there are only three dance steps. Those three steps are forward, backward, and side. Any dance figure that social dancers use is made up of these three directions and you have already learned to do them with quality and poise!

OK, we must get back to our lesson. Do you remember our lesson on the timing of the dance steps? If not, please review that section right now. Thank you.

The FOXTROT

Since we used the count of Slow for all of our forward and backward steps in practice, we will continue to use the Slow count for these steps in your first dance, the Foxtrot. The side and closing steps, our common denominator to all of our future figures will be done in the dance timing of Quick for the side step and Quick for the closing step.

- Therefore the Forward Half Box will be counted as follows: Slow-Quick-Quick.

- The Backward Half Box will be counted as follows: Slow-Quick-Quick.

I know you are still next to each other and both of you want to get back into your dance frame as a couple, but please wait for a minute more.

I'll compromise with you, please take your partner's hand and we will begin to practice the Dancer's Square Step, otherwise known as the Box Step, together in side by side position. I want you to count aloud as follows; "Slow-Quick-Quick." Then begin to move. Please continue to count aloud, "Slow-Quick-Quick." Use as many of the combined Forward and Backwards Half Box Steps as necessary to get you and your partner dancing the square in perfect unison.

You see I want you to be able to dance by yourself to make the moment you dance together wonderful and effortless! **Remember a Slow count is 2 increments or beats of music and a Quick is only 1 increment or beat of music.** Each of the Half Box Steps will take a total of 4 beats while using only 3 steps. The full Square Step will take a total of 8 beats while using only 6 steps.

Continue to practice while holding hands and practice until you are synchronized with your partner and moving approximately the same distance in stride.

I hope you have some music available and that it's in the CD format. Please find your Foxtrot selection and put on the music in the repeat mode.

Begin to dance in side by side position, while holding hands, and counting aloud until you, your partner, and the music are completely synchronized. CONGRATULA-TIONS, you are indeed dancing and have reached the mountain top. This is the hardest lesson in the Quickstart to Social Dancing program. The rest is all downhill!

Leg Swing Can Vary
From Body Direction

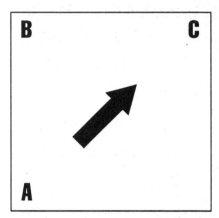

The arrow indicates leg swing.

- I have prepared a diagram to show my students that the swing of the leg can vary from the final position of the foot.

- In the case of a body weight change on a sideways step that was preceded by either a forward or backward step, you will find that your leg will swing in a diagonal direction. Please do not let this confuse you.

- The direction you traveled with your body is all that is important. At the conclusion of the body weight change you will find you have placed your foot to the side of your last foot placement. **In dancing we measure that direction from where we were standing or where the standing foot was.** The leg may have swung diagonally, but the foot placement ended side on the same plane of the other foot.

In the diagram on the preceding page I have shown that the right foot will travel from Position A to Position C on a Forward Half Box in any of the Dances using the Box or Square Step pattern. The arrow indicates the way the right leg swings to the final foot Position C. Therefore Position C was to the side of Position B regardless of the leg swing.

Advanced Technique of the Closing Step

It may be that the closing step still offers a bit of a challenge. To give you an edge for the Foxtrot and the five remaining dances I want to add more insight into the technique we have discussed. I would consider this technique advanced but it will definitely help you at the beginner level. Three things must happen in sequence when you close one foot to another. All three happen on just one beat of music, they are:

• The swing or placement next to the supporting foot

• The transfer of weight to the moving foot after the swing and placement of the closing foot.

• The release of the supporting from the floor.

As a result, my recommendation is:
Whenever you close the feet do it without the least bit of hesitation. Simply said, "As quickly as possible."

The following is a habit you do want in your dancing:

- If you are one of my older readers you may have been exposed to another unsuccessful method of teaching dance from the "Good Old Days." A teacher would show a form of the Waltz Box Step or Foxtrot Box Step that was used by European teachers from another era. They tried to use an old fashioned figure from what was known as the Hesitation Waltz.

- This figure was a moving step followed by a touching step so that the feet always finished next to each other. This was useful when all of the Waltz music was twice as fast as the present tempo used in the Waltz to which we currently dance. These were the old European Viennese or Strauss Waltzes. The music was so fast that many people had to employ this hesitation method of dancing to keep up with the music.

- Unfortunately certain methods of teaching did not keep up with the times. Your grandmother could have been shown this step touch method by her mother and passed it forward to your mother, etc.

- In today's dancing there is no benefit gained by moving a leg forward to the standing foot then moving it to the side to finish the step. This type of action may have already confused you in the past, so let us start freshly with no random or arbitrary use of the leg or foot.

Dancing Foxtrot With A Partner

Now you'll be able to dance to the wonderful ballad rhythms of Damone, Cole, Darin, Sinatra, and Connick to name a few.

Continuing Lesson 4 with the Foxtrot

I have already described the dance position and frame of the couple so I want you to please get into dance position with your partner. Reread and review that section if necessary.

- **The gentleman will begin with the Forward Half Box Step and the woman will begin with the Backward Half Box Step.**

The lady's right foot should be free of body weight and the gentleman's left foot should be free to move.

The gentleman will bring his partner into the music by counting aloud, "Slow-Quick-Quick." While slightly flexing his right knee so as to begin movement with his partner. Both the man and the lady are now counting aloud, "Slow-Quick-Quick." They are using the same music they used earlier when they were side by side.

JEFF SAYS:

"It is never appropriate or correct to exaggerate distance with your feet. A better idea is to keep your body moving with the feet under it."

Foxtrot begins following this
arrow: slow, quick, quick

**To continue and conclude
the Box Step the gentleman
will use the Backward Half
Box Step and the lady will
use the Forward Half Box
Step while continuing the
same count of Slow-Quick-
Quick.**

- This should be very easy because you have done this
  before.

- Make no attempt to vary the quality of your movement
  by stepping off your tightrope.

- Invite each other into your space and please do not look
  down at your feet or the floor.

- This will spoil everything. Instead, make a conscious
  effort to move as if no one is in front of you, just as you
  did during your side by side practice session.

- Remember when you were walking with each other in
  closed position, you were learning to trust your
  partner's ability to move themselves away from or
  towards you.

- Ladies, his job is never to use any strength whatsoever
  to cause or create movement for you in any direction.

- If you maintain a feeling of lift from your little bottom and your rib cage, you'll do a good job.

- Study the section on the couple's frame once again to make sure you are doing it correctly.

Practice for Success

Please continue to practice the Full Box Step over and over to the Foxtrot Rhythm of Slow, Quick, Quick, Slow, Quick, Quick. Once you are moving with normal stride and no lurching or pulling exists you are ready to proceed to the next lesson. You and your partner are ready to take your Foxtrot Box out for a little dining and dancing. Congratulations.

This is the end of Lesson 4 .

From this point on, things are going to get easier!

LESSON FIVE:
Waltz

**We are going to learn the Waltz and the Rumba. The
good news is you have already done the hard work.**

Great news! The Waltz Box Step and the Rumba Box
Step are exactly the same as the Foxtrot Box Step. In the
Waltz there is an easy to learn tempo or rhythm change
and in the Rumba there is a minor difference in the type
of foot placement. Neither of these differences will pose
any great difficulty to my students. You have already done
the hard part, and I will help you with the differences to
make them easy.

Let us proceed with the Waltz as your second dance.

In our previous lesson about timing or rhythm we learned
that a Quick is one increment or beat of music. Waltz
music is comprised of three beats to the bar of music otherwise known as $^3/_4$ timing. In Foxtrot we were dancing to
$^4/_4$ timing.

**This is the
beginning of
Lesson 5A.**

**I want you
to take a
moment to
listen to
the Waltz
selection
on your CD.**

The beginner dancer, only needs to know that in Waltz, every step of the Waltz Box will be taken at the same speed. We will use the counting cadence of either 1-2-3. Or, to remain consistent with our other dances, we will use Quick-Quick-Quick as our counting cadence.

You will hear the consistency of the tempo. Count with it aloud using either 1-2-3 or Quick-Quick-Quick. If you are fond of mathematics you have figured out that a Quick increment in the Waltz has to be danced a little slower than a Quick increment in the Foxtrot. This occurs when the music is played at the same tempo. A Quick increment in the Waltz is just a bit faster than a Slow increment in the Foxtrot.

Most people think the Waltz is easier to negotiate than the Foxtrot; I agree. This fact should be a great confidence builder for you. I told you that you were at the top of the mountain. The reason I showed you the Foxtrot first is because Foxtrot rhythm is much more popular in musical composition than Waltz is. Let's say you had decided to go out for some dinner and dancing after Lesson 4 you would get more usage out of the Foxtrot than you would the Waltz.

OK Dancers, simply employ the use of the Forward Half Box and the Backward Half Box with the new rhythm of Quick- Quick-Quick.

This would be exactly the same as you did in Lesson 4 of the Foxtrot. You and your partner are on the way to dancing the Waltz. I just want to stress our common denominator, the closing step, one more time. Make sure that when your feet close together (see: Closing the Feet) that you instantly release the supporting foot from the floor. In so doing you will produce a smooth transition to the next position and will not trap both of your feet under your body. Remember the advanced technique I told you about (see: Page 50).

The Waltz Square or Box Step is now complete. Count aloud with your partner and the music, and begin to enjoy the wonderful, romantic, dreamy quality of the Waltz.

JEFF SAYS:

"Never finish a Dance Step or Figure with weight on both feet."

To Review Lesson 5A

Here is another easy diagram to help you review Lesson 5A

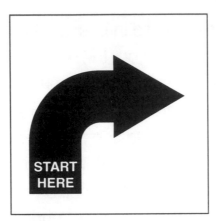

Waltz: begins following this arrow. **Counting:** quick, quick, quick, or 1, 2, 3

Practice for Success

By now you should have developed a good practicing scenario from the use of your previous lessons: Here are some quick reminder hints:

1. **Repeat your step patterns aloud.**
2. **Count for you and your partner aloud.**
3. **Develop good rhythm with your pattern while apart from each other.**
4. **Once you have taken the Dance Position, do not change your feeling or movement.**

Continue to practice your Waltz Box Step together until you and your partner are perfectly synchronized.

Do not forget that on a CD player you have that wonderful repeat button.

Here is a Word of Advice
to the Bride & Groom.

If you have just received this book and there are only a couple of weeks before the wedding, please do the following. After this section is completed, please skip to the section about the Script. Once you soon-to-be-newlyweds have gone through and practiced **the Presentation of the Bride and the Couple's First Dance,** you may have time to return to the book and complete the lessons. Completing the lessons in this book will provide for more fun at your own reception or honeymoon. We must consider priorities at this time. The first dance of the bride and groom and possibly the dance of the bride and the person who presented her at the ceremony is your prime focus now.

To see if you are really ready for that "Big Day" or "Your First Dance," I want you to select a Foxtrot and then a Waltz and dance to them in succession. Do this over and over again. It is important that you become extremely familiar with both of these rhythms. You will need to be, when choosing your first song. I know this is very important to you. Select a song that matches either of these two rhythms perfectly rather than a very slow ballad. A slow ballad might be beautiful to listen to, but it really takes an expert to dance to one. **One way to discover what songs are out there in the tempo you desire is to visit our Internet website. We have posted an extensive library of wedding songs. The URL is http://home.earthlink.net/~dancebook/.** Disc jockeys, radio stations, music stores, musicians, relatives and friends who are experienced dancers are also alternative sources for information about song selections. At the conclusion of this text I have featured a list of some timeless favorites that you may wish to consider for your first dance. They will certainly provide you with good examples of dance rhythms.

OK, Everyone, Back to the Lesson

As I mentioned to the engaged couple it is a good idea to practice your Waltz and Foxtrot alternately.

- This will guarantee you can distinguish between the rhythms of the music and therefore the timing of the Dance Steps.

- Dancing is predominantly a physical skill, not just an intellectual skill. Repetition and saturation are most important at this beginner level.

- For those of you who feel you have no rhythm I have to tell you that rhythm in anything is an acquired skill. Everyone has a different learning curve or acquires skills in different increments of time, but everyone must learn. Every single physical endeavor you participate in and repeat on a daily basis whether at home, work, or driving your car requires rhythm. In order to write, eat, climb a staircase, or shift a car, rhythm is necessary.

- Counting aloud with the music as you are learning to dance with your partner will teach you rhythm. I have heard all the excuses before, and I have trained people to dance who claimed to be my worst students of all time. I thought it was time for my little sermon right about now.

REMEMBER:

**Count Aloud
with the
Music.**

The Rumba: The Dance of Love and Sensuality is Waiting for You.

We are ready to learn the Rumba Square, also called the Rumba Box Step. The timing of the Rumba and the directional pattern are essentially the same as the Foxtrot. I want you to do it with just a couple of minor alterations that will lay down a foundation that will make things easier and more attractive when you go beyond this book. On both counts, I bet you knew I was going to say that!

Some Changes Necessary for a Latin Dance...

Before I tell you about the two minor differences, I want to tell you about some significant changes in foot placement and the leg action used in all of the following Latin dances. I always like to start with the Rumba first because it is the foundational Latin dance. The other two Latin dances we will cover will be the Merengue and the Cha-Cha. All three enjoy enormous popularity and are danced frequently at all social occasions.

Three Dances All Use Similar Foot Placement and Leg Action.

Comparing the Smooth Dances to the Latin Dances...

In the two previous dances the Foxtrot and the Waltz our leg action and foot placements were similar to the way we walk while using good posture and poise. The action of moving backwards in these two dances was the exact reciprocal of moving forward.

• In the Foxtrot and Waltz, when your leg swung it straightened. The foot placement was Heel-Ball-Toe going forward; and Toe-Ball-Heel going backwards.

• You will notice that the knees have a slight flex in them as the body weight passes over the feet. This happens quite naturally when we walk or when we dance Foxtrot or Waltz.

• The result of this type of leg action and foot placement is continued progressive traveling around the dance floor or progression around city streets while walking.

The Latin Dances are designed for small areas with a high population on the dance floor.

The differences between leg action and foot placement in Latin Social Dancing and Smooth American Social Dancing

- These three dances do not travel around the dance floor. Latin Americans love dancing so much their dance floors are always crowded. This love is shared equally by men and women. Gentlemen from Latin American countries feel a person is not "macho" if he cannot dance. It is their culture, and they respect it with reverence. So when you visit their nightclub establishments you will understand this and will know how to dance comfortably and in character.

- In a Latin dance the leg swings with pre-established flex in the knee and then straightens as the body weight is brought onto the feet.

- The foot placement is always done with the ball of the foot first and then the foot becomes flat as the body weight continues onto and downward into the feet.

- This form of foot placement and knee-leg action resembles both traveling up or down a staircase and pedaling a bicycle. I know you can all do this, so please no moaning or excuses about this different method. **Remember smooth dances as the Waltz or Foxtrot are walking dances. Latin dances like Rumba, Cha-Cha, and Merengue are staircase dances.** Try climbing a staircase at this point and you will have the technique down perfectly. Remember I am using the staircase and bicycle as illustrations. It is not necessary to do either when learning how to dance.

- There is also an added benefit to the staircase method of movement. Without doing anything special there is hip flex or what dancers call Latin or Cuban motion of the hips when anyone ascends a staircase. There is absolutely no need to do anything but the staircase method of leg action to produce suitable movement of the hips! The same leg and hip motion are true while you are motoring a bicycle. Never, never wiggle your hips; the knee flexing is what experienced dancers use for that sensuous Latin motion.

SMOOTH DANCES:

Waltz
Foxtrot

STAIRCASE DANCES:

Rumba
Cha-Cha
Merengue

The Rumba Box is Slightly Different

Now we must cover the two minor differences in the timing and starting direction of the Rumba Square Step.

- The timing will start with the Quick, Quick increments being done first, followed by the Slow increment.

- The second difference, to accommodate the first change, is we will start with the side step and the closing step prior to either the forward or backward step.

- In the case of the Rumba, the Forward Half Box will be done side step, closing step, forward step.

- As you would expect the Backward Half Box will be done side step, closing step, backward step.

- All of these steps include the staircase method of foot placement, ball then flat, and the leg actions of flex then straighten. That's it. The Rumba Square, otherwise known as the Rumba Box Step, is complete!

To get into your couple's frame use the same procedure as you did for the previous dances. Please begin to dance the Rumba.

Please note that the instruction, "Close," is an abbreviation of the instruction we have called the Closing Step.

- The gentleman with the left foot free of body weight, will begin side, close, forward followed by side, close, backward.

- The lady with the right foot free of body weight, will begin side, close, backward, followed by side, close, forward.

- Do not forget to count aloud, "Quick, Quick, Slow; Quick, Quick, Slow." **Another method of counting when we first started the Quickstart to Social Dancing Program was to rhythmically say the directions we were traveling.** In the case of the Rumba we would count as follows; side, close, step, side, close, step. This seems to help many new dancers.

- By now you should be used to trying the dance at first facing each other without contact with Rumba music playing and then joining your partner in your dancer's frame.

JEFF'S 11TH COMMANDMENT OF DANCE:

"Once we have completed a movement to the side (i.e., a Side Step), quickly draw the free foot to a close and immediately put ALL your weight on that closing foot!"

The following is your simplified diagram of the starting direction and timing of the Rumba. Please note the changes from the Waltz diagram.

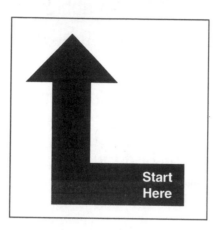

Rumba begins following the arrow—moving side, close, step. The count is quick, quick, slow.

This is the end of Lesson 5 B.

Congratulations. You have now completed three of the dances in the Quickstart to Social Dancing Program. They are three of the most popular dances in the world and will provide you with many hours of social enjoyment and pleasant exercise while you practice.

Once you have learned a dance, please practice in short spurts of time. This should be no more than 15 minutes per practice session. The catch to quick and easy learning along with confidence is **saturation**, you must practice daily.

You cannot stop now. We still must learn three more dances. But you must admit the lessons are getting easier to understand and shorter in time duration.

Are you planning a cruise or possibly a vacation to a
warm climate? Is this a first or second honeymoon?
If so, then you have to learn the following dance, THE
MERENGUE. This one is very easy and is HOT, HOT,
HOT (you know the song).

LESSON SIX:
The Merengue

It is possible that on any given weekend evening more people are dancing to the Merengue beat than any other dance in the world.

- The Merengue has a very simple timing structure.

- Each Step Pattern is danced to 8 beats or increments of music.

- We dance a complete weight change on every single beat and use the counts of 8 Quicks in a row.

- The Merengue is a Latin dance so we implement **Latin leg action and foot placement** as previously described in the Rumba.

- Except for a minor accommodation to account for 8 beats or increments of music we have completely covered the basic movements of the Merengue.

The first step pattern that is coincidental to the Merengue and that we have covered was done in the very first practice lesson.

Do you remember the side steps followed by the closing steps? If not, will you please review that lesson at this point. OK, we are now ready to continue.

**I hope you remember we called this type of action a
chassé step. Do a good job with it because it will be
used again in the Swing and the Cha-Cha.**

In that first lesson we moved sideways by stepping to the
side and then closing our feet.

This was done for a total of 4 complete sets equal to
8 Quicks.

Now all you have to do is apply the Latin elements and
begin to move sideways with your partner. The man will
begin with his left foot free moving to the left. The lady will
do the natural opposite. We will call this figure the
Merengue Chassé.

I want to help you stylize your Merengue Chassé.
However, this will take a little bit of time to become comfortable. This small section is optional at first, but soon
you will want to implement these additions.

- The knees will remain closer together than the feet on
  the Merengue Chassé

- The left knee of the man will lift a little higher than the
  right knee. The opposite is true for the woman

- The man places the inside edge of the big toe and the
  ball of his left foot on the dance floor first. The lady will
  strike with the inside edge of the big toe and the ball of
  her right foot.

The dance
term chassé
comes from
the French
word
chase—
one foot
chasing the
other.

71

- To produce the appropriate rolling of the feet, dance as if you are trying to point your ankle bones at the floor rather than towards each other.

The end result of this stylization of the Merengue Chassé

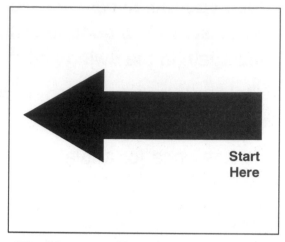

The Merengue Chassé begins following this arrow. The count is 8 quicks.

will produce a feeling or action that attempts to hug the lady's right knee between the gentleman's knees. The Merengue is a sexy little dance, so don't be afraid to get closer to your partner.

Here is More You Can Do With the Merengue Chassé

What could be more simple than moving for 8 Quicks to the man's left by opening and closing the feet?

- Well, it actually does get simpler because you can actually do the Merengue Chassé in place or in place turning in a very small circle.

- In place or in place turning is actually a more authentic Latin form of the Merengue Chassé.

• I am sure you remember that Latin American Dancing is generally done on a very crowded dance floor in very small spaces.

The Dance of Merengue can be done to extraordinarily fast Merengue music. I have brought this point up to tell you beginner dancers that there is a common oversight made when practicing a Chassé.

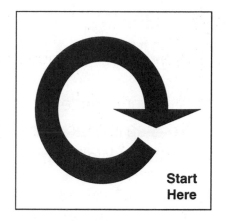

The Merengue Chassé can be danced in place or in a small circle following this arrow. The count is 8 quicks.

The closing action is often done too slowly by beginners.

• It is a better idea to speed up the closing action whenever the dance figure you are doing calls for it. In this way you will probably just get it done in time.

• I often tell my students to do the chase in the chassé or close the foot as fast as possible. This advice will serve you well in every dance you do.

By now you can probably begin in closed position or the dancer's frame with the music playing! GREAT!

The Merengue Box Step is The Second Major Pattern.

The directional pattern used to do the Merengue Box or Square Step is exactly the same as the directional pattern used with the Waltz Square or Box Step.

• In the Waltz we used both the Forward Half Box Step and the Backward Half Box Step for a total of 6 body weight changes.

• We counted this Waltz Box Step for a total of 6 Quicks.

• I said earlier each pattern in the Merengue has a total of 8 body weight changes counted for a total of 8 Quicks.

• Using the Latin leg action and foot placement technique we will step in place with no progression for 2 more Quicks.

• This happens at the conclusion of the Merengue Square or Box Step.

• Just remember, when dancing the Merengue, it is 6 plus 2.

• Some dancers count 1 through 8 for a total of 8 Quicks.

• Others count repeating aloud, "Forward Half Box;" "Backward Half Box;" and then say, "In Place-In Place."

The Diagram of the Merengue Box Step

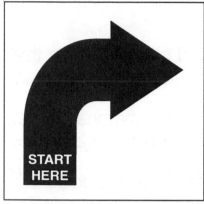

The Merengue Box:
Forward half box followed
by backward half box followed
by in place-in place.

Begin following the
direction of the arrow.

Count for a total of 8 quicks.

Congratulations, you have now completed 4 of the most popular dances done all over the world today.

• Increase your practice time to include the Foxtrot, Waltz, Rumba and now the Merengue.

• Get familiar with the music and count aloud for your partner to increase the ease of understanding and hearing your dance rhythm.

Gentlemen, when beginning a dance do not try to bring you partner into motion by starting from a straight leg and just moving your foot.

- What you must do is count aloud something like this: "5-6-7-8 and," or "5-6-ready-go."

- In addition to this counting please remember to flex your knees on either the "8-and" or the "ready-go."

- In this way both of you will bring your bodies into motion.

- This will give you a nice smooth start.

- If you just wait for the music to begin you will find that you actually start behind the music because of its consecutive and ongoing nature.

That is why I say, "You must bring your partner into the music." Good luck and let's get ready for the next lesson.

LESSON SEVEN:
The Swing and the Cha-Cha

We complete our six dance, Quickstart to Social Dancing Program with the Swing and the Cha-Cha. These are two of the most popular dances in the World.

In my opinion the Swing is the most popular dance and actually has a family of dances with differing variations.

We will cover the most popular variety that is known as the Swing, Triple Swing, or East Coast Swing. All three names are synonymous.

In spite of the Swing's popularity I have waited to this point in the Quickstart to Social Dancing Program to introduce it to you because of the physical logic that makes up the Swing's characteristic.

To keep a logical progression in the Quickstart to Social Dancing Program I wanted to make sure that my students have already executed all of the components of the Swing.

In this way, a dance that would otherwise have been difficult to start with, will be much easier at this point.

The Beginning of Lesson 7A.

Swing=

Triple Swing=

East Coast Swing

You have already learned all of the terminology and done all of the figure types in the Swing.

This should allow you to begin this dance with a lot of confidence.

The chances are you will use this dance more than any other, particularly if you are fond of nightclubs and parties.

LET'S BEGIN TO SWING

The elements of the Swing are 2 Chassés consisting of three weight changes. These Chassés are followed by a body weight change backwards and a body weight change forwards. This pattern is done exactly the same for the gentleman and the lady. We will divide the Swing into three units of 2 beats or 2 increment units of music.

OK. We Are Ready for the 1st of the Three Swing Units.

The 1st unit is a three step chassé moving to the gentle-man's left and to the lady's right.

From the section on moving sideways and from the last dance we covered, the Merengue, you have learned how to do a Chassé. Just in case you have forgotten, let us review this abbreviated form of the Merengue Chassé that is done with only three body weight changes.

The gentleman will start with his body weight on the right foot. The lady will do the natural opposite.

Each will flex both knees upon beginning the movement.

Note that when dancing the Swing both knees will always have some degree of flex in them.

This knee flex is like a very soft bounce action of a pogo stick or diving board.

You never fully straighten your legs while doing the Swing.

• You can tell if you are over straightening your legs if your ankles lock.

• Locking your ankles will take the rhythm out of the Swing.

The Swing is thought to be the most rhythmic of all the dances, "It don't mean a thing if it ain't got that Swing!"

When you are in a nightclub doing what we call freestyle dancing you never lock your ankles. In one sense both freestyle and swing dancing seem to never finish. Those folks who persist in locking, or fully straightening their ankles, produce an undesirable mechanical or robotic look. I know you do not want that!

• The gentleman will move his body approximately ten inches to the left until his weight is over the left foot.

• The ball of the foot will strike the floor first and then the whole foot will finish. Remember the soft bounce that starts downward first.

   (The lady will do the natural opposite).

• The gentleman will use our Chassé closing action with the right foot. Remember both knees will flex with a soft bounce. (The lady will do the natural opposite).

• The gentleman will repeat the action of moving ten inches to his left (The lady will do the natural opposite).

• The counting of these three body weight changes is Quick-Quick-Slow. In the case of the Swing a Quick is $\frac{1}{2}$ beat of music and a Slow is 1 full beat of music.

This completes the 1st Unit of the Swing. We will call this 1st Unit a Left Foot Chassé for the man and the lady's action was a Right Foot Chassé.

The 2nd Unit of the Swing is exactly the natural opposite of the 1st Unit.

The gentleman now moves to his right counting, "Quick-Quick-Slow." So in this case the man has done a Right Foot Chassé while the woman has done a Left Foot Chassé. Please do not forget the soft bounce action!

This Right Foot Chassé having been done by the man and the Left Foot Chassé having been done by the woman completes the 2nd Unit of the Swing.

The last of our three units is what we will call the Swing Rock.

- The Swing Rock consists of a soft bounce action of the knees with the body moving backward and then immediately forward.

- The distance the dancer will travel backward and forward is the length of the dancer's foot. More than this will produce a yanking and pulling action on your partner's hand or body and this is simply very bad dancing. You should never do anything while dancing to pull on your partner's hand so as to affect their upper body. This sling shot action occurs only if the dancers are losing their balance. Regardless of what you may see on the social dance floor, my students will not pull on their partner!

• The man makes a body weight change back to the left foot while lifting his right foot in place approximately two inches from the floor. When lifting your foot from the floor keep the sole of the foot parallel to the dance floor.

• He then immediately moves his body weight forward over the right foot. This action resembles marching in place to mark time with slight body movement and of course the soft bounce. The lady will also move her body backwards over her right foot and recover immediately to her left.

The counting for the Swing Rock is "slow-slow," or 1 full beat back and 1 full beat forward.

The position of the dancer's frame can be done as previously described in Lesson 2, "Embracing Your Partner," or with the following minor difference. Many dancers will vary the closed position frame by allowing the gentleman's left hand to receive the lady's right hand downward in a position similar to holding hands while walking. This is done while the couple remains in closed position allowing the arms to freely drop down just below their former position.

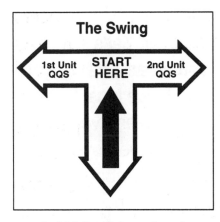

3rd Unit backward and
forward rock, slow, slow

Alternatives to this closed position can be a single hand hold which would be the gentleman's left hand to the lady's right hand or a double hand hold. In both single and double hand holds the arms are relaxed downward at full extension.

The gentleman's hand is under the lady's hand. The hand connection of the partners remains equidistant or centered from both partners. This is similar to holding hands while walking. The right hand and arm of the gentleman are released from his partner's back and the lady's left hand and arm are released from her partner's right shoulder.

These positions are called Open Facing positions because there is no body contact.

I want you to be able to dance the Swing in an area of no greater than 25 square feet (5' X 5', etc.).

This is very important particularly when you are in the midst of many people on the dance floor. Let's say on a crowded nightclub dance floor you hear one of your favorites and you want to try out your dance legs. It would be very improper to bump into other couples even if they are just free-style dancing. Some folks have never taken dance lessons or been given sound advice about partner dancing. They proceed to get out on the dance floor and mimic something like the Swing or Jitterbug. This type of couple creates a physical threat to themselves and all who are dancing around them. They do something I call slingshot jitterbug only in this case they are the shot or the stone flying around out of control looking to cause damage. Remember you should never have to yank or pull on your partner, particularly if you have mastered the Swing Rock.

We are going to try a simple underarm turn. We will call the turn a loop turn.

Now that you have established your 5' X 5' square dance space I want the gentleman to take his partner's right hand with his left hand. You are now going to change places with each other. This is how you will do it.

• The lady will pass very close by the gentleman with her back passing in a parallel position in front of his chest.

• To cut down the distance required to do this both the gentleman and the lady will be moving.

• While this happens the gentleman will loop his forearm over the lady's head and then drop the loop immediately once his forearm has cleared her head.

• This forearm passage over her head will be similar to the action of a jump rope.

• The automatic response will be to turn enough to face each other. This is very easy, right?

OK, now that you have done the hard part we simply have to add the three units of the Swing to the recipe.

- You will have to dance this underarm figure with the single hand hold of the man's left hand to the lady's right hand.

- You will be facing each other while dancing the basic Swing pattern as described above.

- The same Swing tempo will always be used. As you know there are 8 body weight changes to complete the basic Swing pattern. For your review they are counted;

  A. Quick-Quick-Slow for the 1st Unit
  B. Quick-Quick-Slow for the 2nd Unit
  C. Slow-Slow for the 3rd Unit (Swing Rock)

- Once the 3rd Unit is complete from the open position (just described above) the man lifts the loop up, not over the lady's head.

- The 1st Unit or the man's Left Foot Chassé and the lady's Right Foot Chassé will be used to pass each other while the loop passes over her head.

- Remember the lady's back passes by the man's chest.

- The loop drops as the couple completes the third step of their Chassé. That would be on the Slow count.

- Both partners will automatically be facing each other once the loop drops.

- Ladies there is no need to duck. I promise he won't hit you in the head. Right, Guys?!

- The 2nd and the 3rd Units will be danced as usual. This will take a little practice. After all, it is the hardest dance figure we have tried together.

Let's try a variation to the loop turn...

If you wish to attempt to dance a variation in the Swing, please try the following.

- Once the loop has dropped you may switch hands. This would be to create a handshake hold with the man and the lady both using their right hands.

- You may attempt a Loop Turn exactly as described above. You may repeat this Loop Turn as many times as you wish changing hands as often as you like.

- The gentleman may return to his partner in a closed dance position, by simply Chasséing towards his partner on the 1st Unit.

- Then he can close the frame on the 2nd Unit. It is not advisable to attempt to close together on the 3rd Unit, the Swing Rock. You would have to lurch forward and yank or pull on each other to close on the 3rd Unit.

A NOTE TO THE GUYS FROM THE TEACHER:

"Gentlemen you must continue to move and keep the tempo of the Swing while doing this Loop Turn. Please do not just stand there waiting for the lady to go by while you admire your work!"

Usage of the Arm in Underarm Turns:

The gentleman's left wrist is the lady's directional guide. When leading a rotation, the man must move his wrist directionally to the area he wants his partner to go. Just moving the arm up is not enough, and I know your intention is not to send the lady to the ceiling.

I generally teach that the first action of any underarm turn is to position the arms of the couple so that they will not impede the couple's progression. The second action is then the directional movement of the man's wrist.

Ladies, a good rule to follow as you continue your dance education is: Always endeavor to keep your elbow under the elevation of the wrist during an underarm turn. Please remember you are passing under his arm and not yours.

This completes your lesson 7A in the wonderful party dance known as the Swing.

The Cha-Cha: The Beginning of Lesson 7B

Congratulations, you have made it to the sixth and final dance of the Quickstart to Social Dancing Program

• The Cha-Cha is a Latin dance utilizing Latin foot placement and leg action.

• The Cha-Cha combines the elements of the three units of the Swing into a diamond shaped figure.

• The basic closed position should be used. However, you may be a bit more comfortable if you are about eight inches from your partner's toes.

• There are two halves to the basic pattern of Cha-Cha and they are counted Slow, Slow, Slow, Quick, Quick ending with the feet together. The actual numeric counting is "1-2-3-4-and." There are five body weight changes in each half of the Cha-Cha basic for a total of ten to complete the diamond shaped basic pattern.

OK. Let Us Begin The Cha-Cha!

As stated several times in the earlier lessons, the gentleman must bring his partner into the music smoothly. This is always done effectively by a very slight flexing action of the knee that is supporting the body's weight.

Counting aloud is of great importance in this dance until it becomes second nature. This is owing to the fact that Cha-Cha music is a bit brisk for beginners and quite sharp or crisp.

We call this type of music Staccato. That means the very first moment of the beat has been shaved off giving the Cha-Cha its most identifiable characteristic.

This characteristic is the Cha-Cha sound on the syncopated fourth beat, counted "4, and," which ultimately named the dance.

A good method for the gentleman to use to bring the lady into the dance would be to count aloud "1-2-3-4-and" while flexing his right knee on the "and" count. The lady will already have her body weight on the left leg and will feel the man's slight knee flex.

- Both the man and the lady will move their body weight to the side, he to the left and she to the right on the 1st count of Slow.

- The distance the body will travel is approximately seven to nine inches and no more.

- This has placed the man's body weight on his left foot and the lady will have her weight on her right foot. This concludes the first of the five body weight changes of the Cha-Cha half basic figure.

I have spent a lot of time describing the opening action of the Cha-Cha because it is difficult.

Students have a bit more difficulty in starting this dance as compared to the others. I am telling you this so you will not become discouraged and feel, as most students do, that you are the worst pupil I have ever had.

Beginning the Cha-Cha 1st Half Basic

- The key to a good beginning is to bring the body into action quickly with a very strong dance frame.

- You must make sure the Atlas and Axis (the joint) at the top of the spinal column moves at exactly the same speed as the Coccyx bone at the base of the spine.

- You must, as in all of our Latin dances, maintain the entire spinal column in a position that is perpendicular to the dance floor. Never bend or lean sideways at the waist to start either the Swing or the Cha-Cha.

The body will not travel well in any linear direction if there is body rock or sway between the waist and the shoulders.

The 2nd and 3rd of the 5 steps is what we could call a Cha-Cha Rock. It is similar to the Swing Rock, but it employs Latin foot placement and leg action.

The 2nd step of the Cha-Cha Basic is a backward step and body weight change for the gentleman and a forward step for his partner. This 2nd Step is the first action of the Cha-Cha Rock.

The 3rd step of the Cha-Cha Basic is an exact replacement of body weight to the spot where that foot was on its previous usage. The previous usage was the position of count 1 that started the basic step. The gentleman will be replacing his weight forward while the lady will be replacing her weight backward. The 3rd step completes the Cha-Cha Rock.

In the Swing Rock Step I told you to release your foot a slight amount from the floor, this is not the case in the Cha-Cha. You must employ what I call a Velcro-like action of the feet especially in the Cha-Cha Rock Steps. Let the feet stick to the floor a little longer until it is absolutely time to move them. If the beginner takes his foot off the floor arbitrarily or too soon, he will not get it back where it belongs. Another pitfall avoided by not using the Velcro action is uncontrolled movement in the shoulders which frequently results from the speedy tempo of much of the Cha-Cha music.

- The gentleman will move his body weight back until it is over his right foot and then forward until the body is over his left foot. The backward and forward movement of the body weight will be counted Slow-Slow.

- The woman will do the natural opposite in that she will do a Cha-Cha Rock with a forward and backward body weight change over her left and then right foot respectively. Of course, the lady is on the exact same count as the man: that is Slow-Slow.

The numeric count of these three of the five opening steps in the Cha-Cha is "1-2-3". Each with a whole increment or beat of music and as in the Swing we count each of them as a Slow.

The 4th and 5th steps are done on the fourth beat of music. Each takes ½ the beat of music and may be counted in any of three ways:

- "Quick-Quick" since a Quick is always ½ the time duration of a Slow.

- "4-and" since this is the actual numeric count in the bar of music.

- "Cha-Cha" since it is fun to say along with the Cha-Cha sound you will hear in the music. Pick one. It is your choice.

The 4th and 5th body weight changes are the same as the Swing or the Merengue side and closing actions.

- The gentleman moves his body to the right and then does a closing action.

- This is done with the right then the left foot leaving the right foot free of body weight, immediately if not sooner.

- As we have learned, the 4th and 5th body weight changes are counted "Quick-Quick" or your choice.

The first half of the Cha-viii

Cha Half Basic is now complete as the feet are both under the body. The lady does the exact natural opposite of her partner.

The 1st Half Basic Step in the CHA-CHA

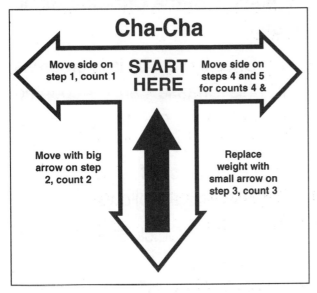

Steps 2 & 3 are the Cha-Cha Rock

The Cha-Cha Chassé

• Since the music has no pause in it, I want to describe the 6th body weight change as the conclusion to what dancers refer to as the Cha-Cha Chassé.

• I can refer to this step as completing a 3 step Chassé movement similar to any 3 steps of the Merengue Chassé or the Swing Chassé.

• In case you have not figured it out yet, that 3rd step is a body weight change to the side.

Remember how you started the Cha-Cha with a side body weight change. This time the man moves his body to the right and the lady moves her body to the left on the 6th step of the Cha-Cha Basic.

Most experienced dancers like the feeling of combining the 4th, 5th, and 6th steps of the Cha-Cha Basic Pattern into a Chassé unit.

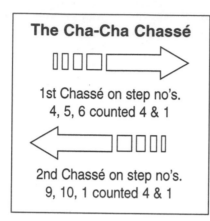

The Cha-Cha Chassé

1st Chassé on step no's.
4, 5, 6 counted 4 & 1

2nd Chassé on step no's.
9, 10, 1 counted 4 & 1

Once the dance is in progress this Chassé can be counted in any of three ways. Remember to count aloud regardless of your choice. They are as follows:

• "Quick-Quick-Slow"
• "4-and-1"
• "Cha-Cha-1"

When thinking of the Cha-Cha in this way, the contents or movements of the Cha-Cha are either a Forward or Backward Cha-Cha Rock followed by a Cha-Cha Chassé.

I hope this simplifies the Cha-Cha. If not, it will in a few short moments. It may also be helpful to divide the Cha-Cha into UNITS as we did in the Swing. You make the choice.

- Returning to our lesson, the 6th step becomes the first body weight change of the 2nd half of the Cha-Cha Basic pattern The 2nd half of the Cha-Cha Basic consists of steps 6-10.

- After completing the closing action, the gentleman continues to move his body to the right until his body weight is over the right foot. He does this on the count of Slow. The lady does the natural opposite.

- 7th and 8th body weight changes comprise a forward Cha-Cha Rock for the man. He will move his body forward over his left foot and backward over his right foot on the count of Slow, Slow. The lady will do a backward Cha-Cha Rock on her right foot and then replace her weight to her left foot.

- The last 9th and 10th body weight changes of the Cha-Cha are comprised of a sideways movement of the body and a closing action of the foot. As you now know, steps 9, 10, and the 1st step of the following pattern complete the second Cha-Cha Chassé displayed in the diagram on page 96.

- The gentleman will move to his left until his weight is over his left foot and then close his right foot to his left foot leaving his left foot free of body weight. This side and closing action will be counted "Quick-Quick." The lady will do the exact natural opposite.

The 2nd Half Basic Step in the Cha-Cha

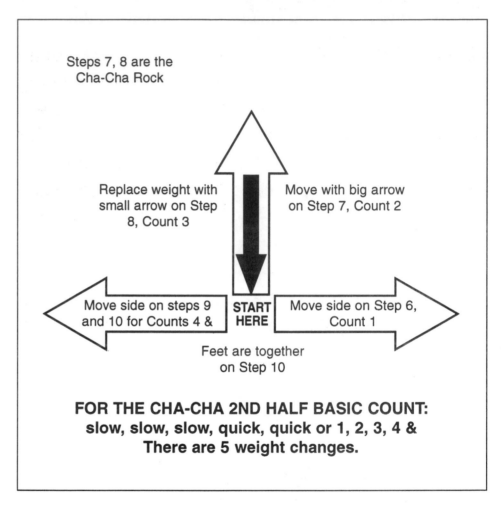

Steps 7, 8 are the
Cha-Cha Rock

Replace weight with
small arrow on Step
8, Count 3

Move with big arrow
on Step 7, Count 2

Move side on steps 9
and 10 for Counts 4 &

**START
HERE**

Move side on Step 6,
Count 1

Feet are together
on Step 10

**FOR THE CHA-CHA 2ND HALF BASIC COUNT:
slow, slow, slow, quick, quick or 1, 2, 3, 4 &
There are 5 weight changes.**

**This Ends
Lesson
7B**

**"It has
truly been a
pleasure to
work with
you. Have a
wonderful
time
dancing!"**

Congratulations. This completes the 10 body weight changes of the diamond shaped pattern known as the Cha-Cha Basic.

Special Section for
the Bride and Groom

Historically the First Dance is symbolic of the consummation of the wedding vows. This dance is the wedding couple's first cooperative engagement and joint endeavor. The newlyweds are placed on the road of life together to fulfill their dreams and aspirations and, more importantly, to complete each other as human beings. When the bride accepts her dance with the groom; she accepts it for the rest of her life. The frame and posture of the groom while he proposes that the bride accept this dance speak of strength, love, companionship, and guidance he offers his bride. It is no wonder that the tradition of the First Dance has continued through history as one of the most important facets of the wedding day. I want to help you make these moments as meaningful and memorable as possible.

Your First Dance as Husband and Wife Should be Memorable and Emotionally Touching.

The Details of the First Dance

Many weddings have no specific plan or time for THE FIRST DANCE during the reception. Consequently, a very beautiful time can come off as haphazard and silly. There are missed opportunities that are regretted in the future. We will not let this happen to you!

The following is a check-off list followed by a SCRIPT for this very special moment at your wedding reception.

1. Have the bride and groom selected their music? For help, refer to our Wedding Song Library at http://home.earthlink.net/~dancebook/

   Did you meet with the orchestra leader or DJ?

   Does the orchestra play your song, and if so in what TEMPO?

   Does the DJ have your title and in what format (CD, etc.)? You may want to have it available.

2. Are the bride and groom prepared to dance to their favorite song?

   How long will they dance together? You may not believe it now, but 2 minutes is a long performance for anyone!

   Who else will be dancing with the bride or the groom? Are they prepared? Will this be danced to a different song?

3. Does the bridal gown have a removable train? Will she hold it in her left hand? Is the dress a full skirt that is capable of being lifted and held with her left hand? You want to be comfortable when the groom has the opportunity to show you off in your beautiful gown while on the dance floor!

   Has the bride practiced walking or dancing in her wedding shoes? This is a good idea. Don't worry; they can be cleaned with solvent or white polish. You do not really want to spend all day in a pair of shoes that have never been worn do you?

   Does the bride's gown give her liberty to move her arms. Do not forget there will be a lot of hugs and kisses that day in addition to dancing. Silk can always be added under the sleeve.

4. Does the groom know if he is wearing patent leather shoes? Patent leather shoes may stick together or squeak. It could be embarrassing if this happens. Therefore, use vaseline on the inner heel to prevent this from happening.

   Does the groom's jacket or enough wing span to dance? He does not want it riding up his neck or splitting under his arms.

5. Does the photographer and/or videographer know you want them ready to shoot your dance sequence?

They need warning both before the wedding day and at the reception.

They often omit this sequence because so many wedding parties are unprepared. Do not let this happen!

The dance sequence is only a few moments. Someone must give them time to set up! Otherwise they'll miss it.

6. The best man is the person whom you can trust to oversee those special needs.

   He is not an employee or someone you have hired. He is someone who will be around in the future and who has pride in being your best man.

   Make the best man aware of each and every thing that is to happen and let him be an overseer of the event. Provide him with the script that will be prepared for your first dance and whatever else may come to mind. He has the role of a man friday or even a bouncer or floor man if necessary.

7. Why is the script important and what are its contents?

   The script is important so the moment of the first dance can be as meaningful and memorable as possible.

   The script will allow for every guest to share in this special moment with the wedding couple.

   The script will allow the photographer and guests to prepare for their picture taking.

The script will make sure the bride and groom have clear access to and use of the dance floor. Sometimes guests have had a bit too much to drink or they may be engrossed in a conversation with someone they have not seen in years. Someone will have to politely ask them to clear the dance floor.

The script will provide for timely and proper announcing of the wedding couple. I know of second and third marriages in which the names in either the introduction for the dance or the toast were given in error. This is BAD!

The script will make sure the music is correct and also timely.

The script will make sure all those participating in the 2nd and 3rd dance will do so and have a proper introduction, (i.e., "Let us bring to the dance floor Mr. John Smith, the Father of the Bride, to join his daughter, etc., etc.").

Presenting the Bride

The following section is a successful formula I have developed and used for instructing my wedding couples through the years. It is designed for maximum effectiveness and emotional impact. There is nothing difficult about presenting the bride. Just follow these simple directions. It will work beautifully for both of you during this very special moment of your wedding day.

The bride and groom enter the room and move to the dance floor. Sometimes you can arrange for an overture or introduction—music for maximum effect in gaining the attention of the room.

1. The bride is to the groom's right. Her left arm is lifted and placed under the elbow and over the forearm of his lifted right arm. The groom's right forearm is parallel to the floor at the level of the bride's bust line.

   Walk forward as described in the first lesson of the Quickstart to Social Dancing Program starting with the groom's left foot and the brides right foot. No Music!

2. The groom escorts the bride to the center of the dance floor and presents her to at least two sides of the room so all of the guest can see her and take photographs. No music!

3. Once this has been done, the groom faces his bride and steps back from her.

 They should pause for a couple of moments adoring each other.

 The families and guests will have to get out their hand-kerchiefs.

4. The groom offers the bride his left hand.

5. NOW THE MUSIC BEGINS!

6. The bride steps forward and accepts the dance of the rest of her life!

7. The couple joins in their dance position and begins their First Dance.

8. NOW, SIGN the Wedding Certificate. Congratulations!

Well, if you have given yourself enough time to practice, this can be a wonderful experience you will remember when helping your children at their wedding. Best of luck!

The Script for Your First Dance

Distribute the script to the MC, the photographer, and the best man before the wedding day.

Make sure all names are accurate and pronounced properly!

Cocktail hour and or remainder of receiving line ends at _____.

5 - 10 minutes before the end of the above have the best man tell the MC, DJ, and or band leader to immediately announce:

• **Ladies and gentlemen, the bride and groom will be making their entrance in just a few short minutes. Please clear the dance floor and the entrance way. If you are going to take pictures, get your cameras ready now. Thank you for your immediate cooperation.**

Have this announcement made again 2-3 minutes before the entrance. The photographer has the equipment ready. The DJ has the music for the entrance (if required) and the FIRST DANCE ready. The 2nd and 3rd dance music is compared to the check-off list and placed in QUEUE.

Have the best man signal the MC, DJ, or band leader when the bride and groom are absolutely ready to make their entrance.

The Announcement:

• Family members and guests, we are very happy and proud to present to you for the first time in public doing their first dance as man and wife, Mr. & Mrs._____.

• Overture is played if required

The bride and groom make their entrance following exactly the advice given to them for the PRESENTATION OF THE BRIDE.

ATTENTION: BAND LEADER OR DJ:

NO MUSIC IS TO BEGIN UNTIL THE BRIDE WALKS FORWARD TO THE GROOM AND THEY TAKE DANCE POSITION!!!

I recommend you dance no more than $1\frac{1}{2}$ - 2 minutes for each of the dances unless you choose otherwise. Instruct the DJ or bandleader to fade music and make announcement for 2nd dance

2nd Dance: Start playing the music while making the announcement

- Let's bring out to the dance floor Mr. _____, the father of the bride, to dance with his lovely daughter_____(first name). This may have to be altered to whomever presented the Bride at the ceremony.

- Fade music and announce the 3rd Dance

3rd Dance: Announcement and play music

- Let's bring out to the dance floor Mrs. _____, the mother of the groom, to dance with her handsome son_____(first name). Alter as required.

- Fade music and announce the 4th dance

4th Dance: Announcement and play music

- Let's bring out to the dance floor Mr. _____, the best man to dance with the Maid of Honor (Miss\Mrs\Ms) _____.

- For any other dances follow the same procedure and make sure all names are announced accurately.

A newer but common tradition is the Exit Dance for the bride and groom. This occurs just prior to the newlyweds departure. You will follow the same procedure as the First Dance but with slightly less formality.

Additional Dance
Figures and Variations...

Now that you have done the basic dance figures, I want to tell you about some simple additions to your repertoire.

The Box Step in 4 of the dances can rotate.

- There is a simple rule you can follow: When the gentleman is stepping forward on his left foot on a Box Step that Box Step can begin to turn LEFT or COUNTER-CLOCKWISE.

- When the gentleman is stepping backwards on his on his right foot that Box Step can continue to turn LEFT or COUNTERCLOCKWISE.

- This often happens automatically owing to the torque in the body if your frame is correct.

- The important thing to know is you may let this happen. This will allow the dance couple to rotate. Nothing changes in your counting.

The Cha-Cha Basic will also rotate counterclockwise.

- Refer to your diagrams on pages 95 and 98.

- This counterclockwise or leftward rotation will occur between Steps number 2,3 on the 1st Half Basic and 7,8 on the 2nd Half Basic. Please remain parallel with your partner during the CHA-CHA Chassé. The rotation will average 1/8 of a circle. Think of a piece of pie.

The Swing Basic can also rotate.

- The Swing Basic will curve rightwards or clockwise.

- The gentleman will naturally curve clockwise around the lady while doing the 1st Unit. Please refer to the diagram on page 83.

- The lady will naturally curve clockwise around the gentleman while doing the 2nd Unit.

- When your partner is curving around you, make your SWING Chassé very small!

- The amount of rotation averages $\frac{1}{4}$ of a circle in the beginning. This amount of rotation can increase with more experience.

Let's Make the Box Step Travel!

Making the Box Step travel is very easy! All that is necessary is to do as follows:

• The gentleman will eliminate his backward movement while doing the Box Step and replace it with a forward movement. This will occur while using his right leg. The side step and closing step will remain the same.

• The lady will eliminate her forward movement and replace it with a backward movement. This will occur while using her left leg. The side step and closing step will remain the same.

• Now the couple can progress around the dance floor. This is particularly useful during the WALTZ and FOXTROT.

Suggested Music for Dancing

Here is a list of songs that have timeless values for your reference. The songs listed in the Foxtrot and Waltz will be suitable for your First Dance.

All these songs are all manageable tempos for beginners. They are placed here to familiarize the reader with the rhythms used for the dances you have studied.

Foxtrot:

It Had To Be You by Harry Connick, Jr.

I Love You by Frank Sinatra

L-O-V-E by Various Artists

Orange Colored Sky by Natalie Cole

Night And Day by Frank Sinatra

Waltz:

Fascination by Jane Morgan

The Sweetheart Tree by Johnny Mathis

Around The World by Jane Morgan

Could I Have This Dance? by Ann Murray

Their Hearts Are Dancing by The Forester Sisters

Rumba:

I Just Called To Say I Love You by Stevie Wonder

It's Now Or Never by Elvis Presley

This Magic Moment by The Drifters

Because by Dave Clark Five

Only The Lonely by Roy Orbison

Merengue:

Hot Hot Hot by Buster Poindexter

Merengue by Various Artists

Conga by Miami Sound Machine

Swing:

Return To Sender by Elvis Presley

Uptown by Roy Orbison

All Around The World by Lou Rawls

The Motown Song by Rod Stewart

Dressed Up To Get Messed Up by Roomful of Blues

Cha-Cha:

Tea For Two by Various Artists

Neon Moon by Brooks and Dunn

Oye Isabel by The Iguanas

Easy Come Easy Go by George Strait